AP 2

AP 24 '18

CAREER EXPLORATION

Licensed Practical Nurse

by Rosemary Wallner

Consultant:
Mary K. James, LPN/DT
President,
National Federation of Licensed Practical Nurses

CAPSTONE BOOKS

an imprint of Capstone Press
Mankato, Minnesota

Capstone Books are published by Capstone Press
P.O. Box 669, 151 Good Counsel Drive, Mankato, Minnesota 56002
http://www.capstone-press.com

Library of Congress Cataloging-in-Publication Data
Wallner, Rosemary, 1964–
    Licensed practical nurse/by Rosemary Wallner
        p. cm.—(Career exploration)
    Includes bibliographical references and index.
    Summary: Introduces the career of the practical nurse through information
about educational requirements, duties, the workplace, salary, employment outlook,
and possible future positions.
    ISBN 0-7368-0329-7
    1. Practical nursing. 2. Practical nursing—Vocational guidance.
[1. Nursing—Vocational guidance. 2. Vocational guidance.] I. Title. II. Series.
RT62.W36 2000
610.73'06'93—dc21   99-24322
                                                                            CIP

Editorial Credits
Leah K. Pockrandt, editor; Steve Christensen, cover designer; Kia Bielke, illustrator;
    Heidi Schoof, photo researcher

Photo Credits
Index Stock Imagery, 24, 46; Index Stock Imagery/Nancy Sheehan, cover; Rick
    Scott (1993), 17; Frank Siteman (1990), 18; Jeff Greenberg, 20; Sally Moskol,
    23 (bottom); Kindra Clineff (1995), 30; Jim Daniels, 41
International Stock/Michael Paras, 23 (top)
Leslie O'Shaughnessy, 14, 36
Photophile/Alan Craft, 9; Tom Tracy, 38
Rainbow/Larry Mulvehill, 6
Unicorn Stock Photos/Eric R. Berndt, 10; Tom McCarthy, 27
Uniphoto, 13; Uniphoto/Charles Gupton, 32

Table of Contents

Fast Facts

Career Title	Licensed Practical Nurse
O*NET Number	32505
DOT Cluster (Dictionary of Occupational Titles)	Professional, technical, and managerial occupations
DOT Number	079.374-014
GOE Number (Guide for Occupational Exploration)	10.02.01
NOC Number (National Occupational Classification-Canada)	3233
Salary Range (U.S. Bureau of Labor Statistics, Human Resources Development Canada, and other industry sources, late 1990s figures)	U.S.: $16,536 to $34,996 Canada: $18,400 to $36,400 (Canadian dollars)
Minimum Educational Requirements	U.S.: associate's degree Canada: diploma
Licensing/Registering Requirements	U.S.: mandatory Canada: mandatory

Subject Knowledge	Customer and personal service; chemistry; biology; psychology; sociology and anthropology; medicine and dentistry; therapy and counseling
Personal Abilities/Skills	Use common sense and medical skills; understand technical information; use eyes, hands, and fingers with skill; work fast in an emergency; communicate with people when they are sick, disabled, or nervous; change from one duty to another frequently; follow instructions exactly; record information accurately
Job Outlook	U.S.: faster than average growth Canada: fair
Personal Interests	Humanitarian: interest in helping others with their mental, spiritual, social, physical, or vocational needs
Similar Types of Jobs	Nurse's aide; emergency medical technician; human service worker; teacher aide

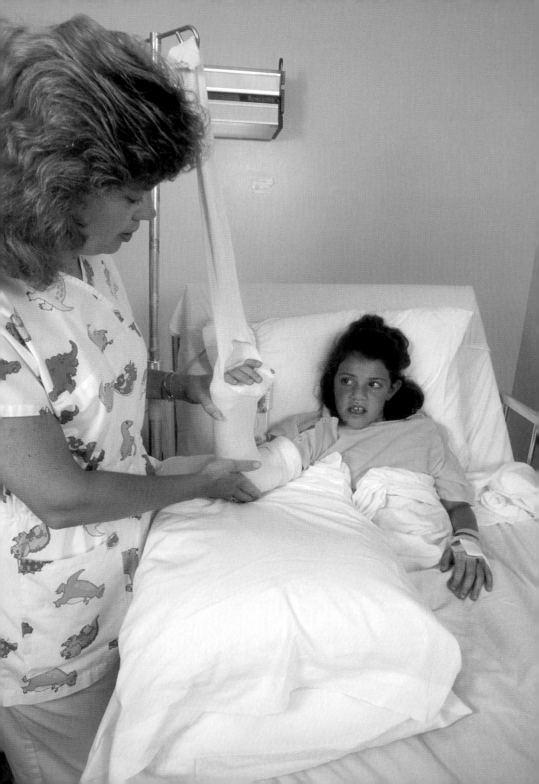

Chapter 1

Licensed Practical Nurse

Licensed practical nurses (LPNs) provide direct nursing care to many types of patients. LPNs take care of people who are sick, injured, or disabled. They also work with patients to prevent illnesses and diseases.

LPNs work in many different settings. They may work in hospitals and clinics. They also may work in long-term care facilities and private homes. Patients stay in long-term care facilities for weeks, months, or even years. A nursing home is a long-term care facility.

Nurses with these duties are not called LPNs in all places. In Texas and California, they are called licensed vocational nurses. In

Licensed practical nurses provide nursing care to many types of patients.

Canada, their titles also may vary. They are called registered nursing assistants in New Brunswick. In Ontario, they are called registered practical nurses. In Quebec, they are called infirmières auxiliaires.

General Work Activities

Licensed practical nurses work under the guidance of doctors and registered nurses (RNs). RNs have more education and training than LPNs.

LPNs mainly provide direct nursing care. They take and record patients' vital signs. These include temperature, respiration, pulse, and blood pressure. Respiration is the process of taking in oxygen and sending out carbon dioxide. Pulse is the throbbing in the veins caused by the heart as it pumps blood. Blood pressure is the measure of the pressure of the blood flow in the arteries. LPNs are taught to recognize unsafe vital signs and act on their findings.

LPNs also observe patients. They tell doctors and RNs how patients react to medications or treatments.

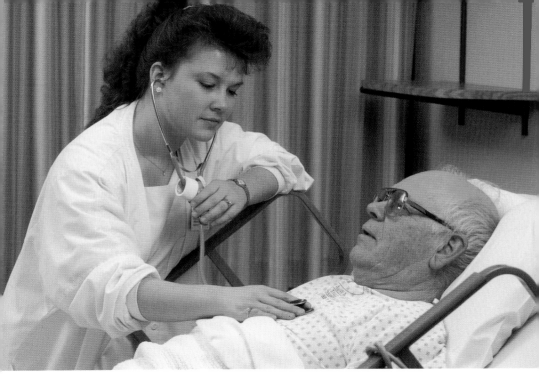

Licensed practical nurses check patients' vital signs.

Other Duties

Licensed practical nurses at hospitals and other health care facilities help patients with basic hygiene. For example, LPNs may help patients take baths and brush their teeth. LPNs also brush patients' hair and help them dress.

LPNs perform simple nursing tasks. For example, they change patients' bandages and apply ice packs to injuries. They also may

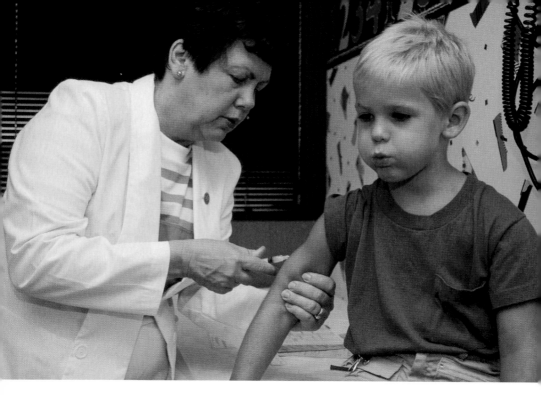

LPNs perform simple nursing tasks such as taking blood samples and giving injections.

collect patient samples such as blood and urine for testing. Some LPNs perform simple lab tests themselves.

LPNs may help medicate patients. For example, they may prepare and give medicine to patients. Medicine can include pills or injections. LPNs inject medicine into patients with syringes. A syringe is a tube with a hollow needle and a plunger. Medicine travels through the needle and into the patient as the LPN presses on the plunger.

LPNs help keep patients comfortable. LPNs talk to patients about their health. This helps LPNs find out what patients need. LPNs feed patients who cannot feed themselves. They help patients get out of bed and walk around. They also massage patients. Massage is the steady pressing and moving of muscles.

Employment Areas

Licensed practical nurses work in a variety of settings. Some LPNs work in hospitals. They provide basic nursing care to patients.

Some hospital LPNs work in specialty areas. These areas may include rehabilitation units, mental care units, or clinics. Rehabilitation units are places where therapists work with patients to overcome disabilities. LPNs in specialty areas receive additional training. They provide direct patient care.

The majority of LPNs work in long-term care facilities. These LPNs provide basic bedside care under the guidance of doctors and RNs. These LPNs also may help develop care plans for patients. Care plans describe treatments and medicines patients need every day.

LPNs also work in clinics. LPNs in clinics prepare patients for medical exams. They weigh patients and check patients' vital signs. LPNs in clinics may even handle office duties. They may answer telephone calls and schedule patients' appointments.

Some LPNs work in private homes. These LPNs sometimes are known as private duty nurses. They care for patients who are well enough to live at home. But these patients still need some care.

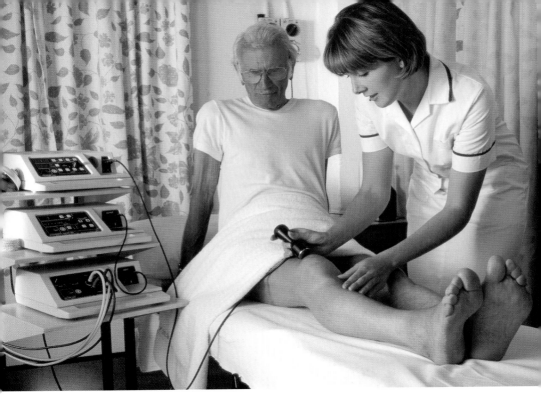

Licensed practical nurses may work in specialty areas such as physical therapy units.

Private duty nurses perform many of the same tasks as LPNs in hospitals and long-term care facilities. Private duty nurses provide day-to-day patient care such as medical treatments and meal preparations. They also may teach family members how to care for patients.

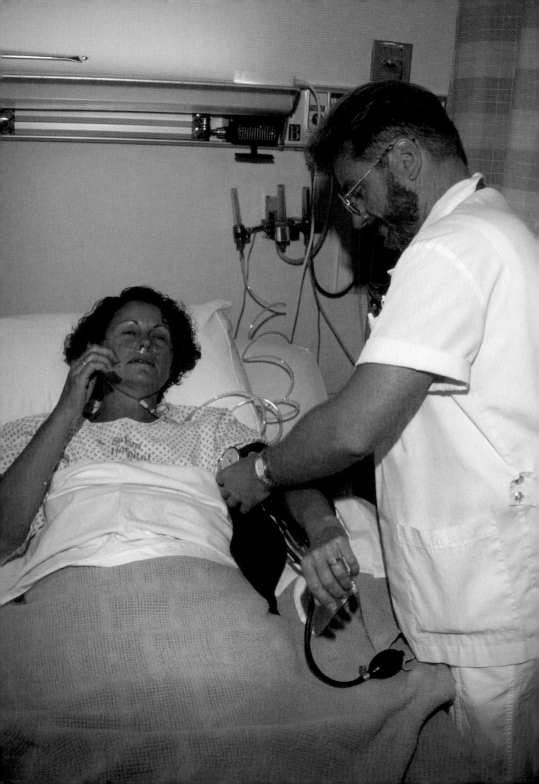

Chapter 2

A Day on the Job

Licensed practical nurses work in a variety of settings. Their daily activities depend on where they work.

LPNs in Hospitals

Licensed practical nurses perform duties assigned by registered nurses. These duties support patients' care plans and doctors' orders. LPNs also observe patients. They report their observations to RNs and doctors.

LPNs in hospitals work hard to make patients comfortable. LPNs start out the day by visiting patients. After breakfast, they help some patients bathe and brush their hair. These nurses need to make sure patients stay clean. For example, they may change a patient's bandages.

Licensed practical nurses observe patients and report their findings.

LPNs also provide routine bedside care. These duties must be done daily. LPNs check patients' vital signs. They prepare patients for medical exams. LPNs record what they do on each patient's chart. This list contains information about a patient, including previous exams, illnesses, and treatments.

LPNs work in many hospital areas. Some LPNs work in maternity units. These LPNs change and dress newborn babies. They teach new mothers how to care for their babies. Other LPNs work in surgery units. They clean surgical tools and arrange them in the operating room. They help doctors and RNs during surgeries. Other LPNs work in pediatric wards. These LPNs help care for babies and young people.

Some hospital LPNs admit new patients. These LPNs ask about patients' medical histories. They find out whether patients are taking any medications. These LPNs ask patients about their symptoms. These physical or mental signs indicate if patients are ill or

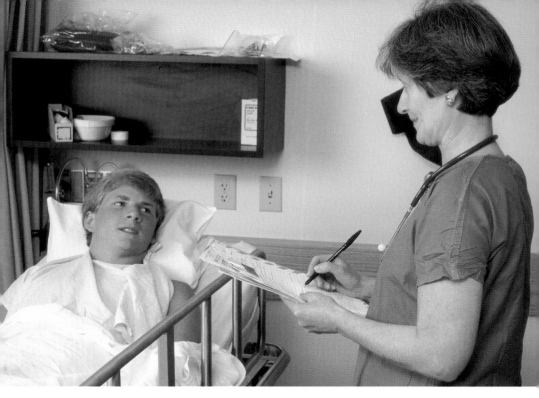

Licensed practical nurses record information about patients on charts.

injured. LPNs write down this information for doctors.

In hospitals, LPNs usually work 40 hours per week. This may include work during nights, weekends, or holidays. Some hospital LPNs are on call. They must be available to work when needed.

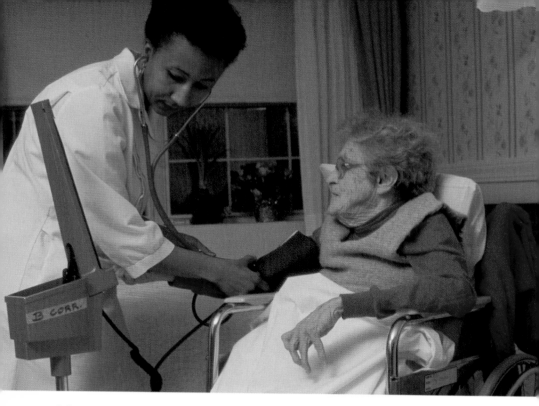

Licensed practical nurses in long-term care facilities are responsible for hands-on care of patients.

LPNs in Long-Term Care Facilities

Many licensed practical nurses work in long-term care facilities. LPNs in these facilities have duties similar to LPNs in hospitals. They also have additional responsibilities. They may provide hands-on care for many patients. Patients in long-term care facilities are called residents. Long-term care residents usually are elderly or disabled. LPNs evaluate residents' needs. They also help to develop care plans for residents. LPNs may supervise nurse's aides.

LPNs work in shifts of about eight hours. These nurses begin a shift by meeting with the LPNs who worked the previous shift. These meetings help LPNs learn about changes in patients' conditions or medications.

LPNs at long-term care facilities go on rounds with doctors. These LPNs and doctors visit each patient. The nurses talk with the doctors about each patient's health and treatment. LPNs update changes in each patient's medication or treatment in a Doctor's Book. LPNs keep track of each patient in this log. This book is also called a Physician's Reference. LPNs also update the Physician Order Sheets. Nurses use these forms to record doctors' medical orders for each patient.

Some LPNs at long-term care facilities oversee units. These LPNs are called charge nurses. Charge nurses oversee the care of every patient in one area of a facility. Charge nurses and nursing assistants perform routine bedside

One of the duties of licensed practical nurses is to record patient information.

care for each patient in that area. Nursing assistants also are called nursing aides, nurse's aides, or hospital attendants.

In long-term care facilities, LPNs work about 40 hours per week. They often must work nights, weekends, and holidays. LPNs with the most experience sometimes may select their work schedules.

LPNs in Clinics

Some licensed practical nurses work in clinics. These LPNs help doctors with patients. LPNs in clinics assist doctors before, during, and after medical exams. These LPNs prepare patients for exams. They weigh patients and check their vital signs.

LPNs may assist doctors during exams. They give bandages or tools such as tweezers to doctors. LPNs also try to keep patients calm during exams. They may stay with patients after exams. LPNs in clinics may give patients information about medicines or how to care for their injuries.

LPNs have other duties at clinics. They may clean exam rooms and wash medical tools the doctors used. LPNs also record information from exams into patients' medical files. They may write comments in patients' charts or enter information into computer files.

LPNs at clinics also perform office duties. They answer phones and schedule appointments for patients. LPNs may call patients to remind them about their appointments. LPNs at clinics keep the patients' files current. They record addresses, phone numbers, and medical histories.

LPNs as Private Duty Nurses

Some licensed practical nurses work as private duty nurses. These LPNs often stay with patients in their homes. Private duty nurses also may visit patients' homes each day or several times a week. Some patients do not need to be hospitalized. But they still may need some care. Private duty nurses stay with patients until the patients do not need this care.

Private duty nurses help patients recover from illnesses or injuries. These nurses provide routine bedside care. They check vital signs and give medications. LPNs also may perform household tasks such as cleaning and laundry. Some LPNs shop and prepare meals for their patients.

LPNs also teach patients' family members how to care for the patients. LPNs teach family members simple nursing tasks. For example, they may teach how to change bandages, take blood samples, or give medicines.

LPNs in Hospitals
These LPNs work under the guidance of doctors and RNs. They provide basic bedside care.

LPNs in Clinics
These LPNs help doctors before, during, and after patients' medical exams. They sometimes file patients' information, make appointments, and answer telephones.

LPNs in Long-Term Care Facilities
These LPNs have more responsibilities than hospital LPNs. In long-term care facilities, LPNs perform basic bedside care. They also help decide patients' treatment and care. Some of these LPNs are in charge of all patients in one area of a facility.

LPNs as Private Duty Nurses
These LPNs often stay with patients in the patients' homes. They also may visit patients' homes each day or several times a week. They assist patients with day-to-day activities. They also teach patients' family members how to care for the patients.

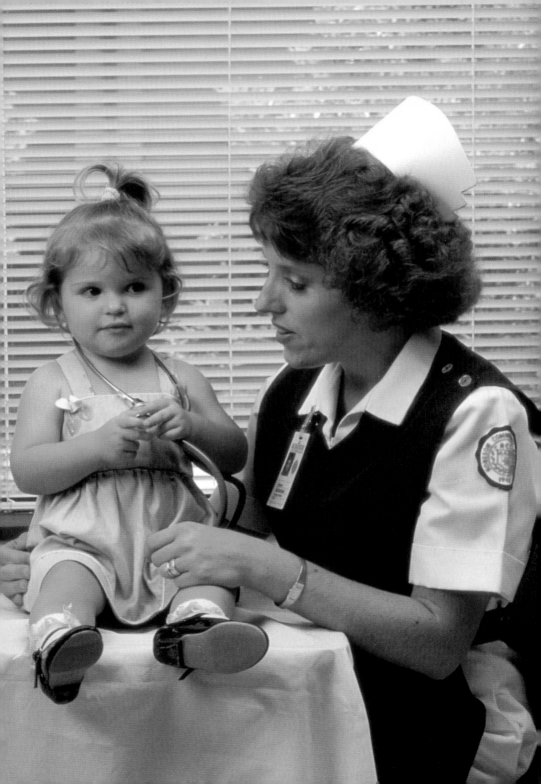

Chapter 3

The Right Candidate

Licensed practical nurses need a variety of skills and interests. LPNs should have an interest in science. They also should work well with people and want to help others.

Abilities

Licensed practical nurses must enjoy helping people. LPNs' main purpose is to look after the well-being of patients.

LPNs must have patience. Sometimes patients are confused, upset, or uncooperative. LPNs must help patients feel calm and comfortable. LPNs also must remain calm during emergencies.

LPNs must be in good health. They must have stamina and physical strength. LPNs must be able to help physically support patients.

Licensed practical nurses must make patients feel calm and comfortable.

LPNs bend, stretch, reach, and lift as they assist patients. LPNs also must be able to stand on their feet for long periods of time.

Skills

Licensed practical nurses should have good communication skills. They must speak with clear voices when they talk with other health care workers. LPNs must understand and discuss instructions for patient care. They also must be good listeners. LPNs need to communicate with patients. They must be able to give correct information to patients and their families.

LPNs must understand technical information. They must know how to use specialized equipment such as stethoscopes. An LPN uses this medical instrument to listen to the sounds of a patient's heart, lungs, and other areas. LPNs must know how to check vital signs and give injections to patients.

LPNs need other basic skills. They must be observant. They need to note patients' reactions to medications and treatments. They must use their hands and fingers with skill. Nurses need to work with exact items such as needles. They

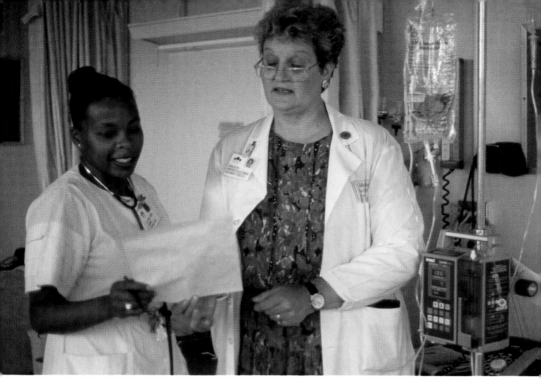

Licensed practical nurses work with other health care professionals on a daily basis.

must be able to work quickly during emergencies. They must be able to switch from one duty to another.

LPNs also must have basic computer skills. They need these skills for many job positions. Most hospitals, clinics, and long-term care facilities train LPNs to perform a few computer tasks. But many health care facilities will not hire LPNs who do not have computer skills.

Skills

Workplace Skills   Yes / No

Resources:
Assign use of time . . . . ☑ ☐
Assign use of money . . . . ☐ ☑
Assign use of material and facility resources . . . . ☑ ☐
Assign use of human resources . . . . ☑ ☐

Interpersonal Skills:
Take part as a member of a team . . . . ☑ ☐
Teach others . . . . ☑ ☐
Serve clients/customers . . . . ☑ ☐
Show leadership . . . . ☑ ☐
Work with others to arrive at a decision . . . . ☑ ☐
Work with a variety of people . . . . ☑ ☐

Information:
Acquire and judge information . . . . . . ☑ ☐
Understand and follow legal requirements . . . . ☑ ☐
Organize and maintain information . . . . . ☑ ☐
Understand and communicate information . . . . ☑ ☐
Use computers to process information . . . . . ☑ ☐

Systems:
Identify, understand, and work with systems . . . . ☑ ☐
Understand environmental, social, political, economic,
    or business systems . . . . ☑ ☐
Oversee and correct system performance . . . . ☐ ☑
Improve and create systems . . . . ☐ ☑

Technology:
Select technology . . . . ☐ ☑
Apply technology to task . . . . ☑ ☐
Maintain and troubleshoot technology . . . . . ☑ ☐

Foundation Skills

Basic Skills:
Read . . . . ☑ ☐
Write . . . . ☑ ☐
Do arithmetic and math . . . . ☑ ☐
Speak and listen . . . . ☑ ☐

Thinking Skills:
Learn . . . . ☑ ☐
Reason . . . . ☑ ☐
Think creatively . . . . ☑ ☐
Make decisions . . . . ☑ ☐
Solve problems . . . . ☑ ☐

Personal Qualities:
Take individual responsibility . . . . ☑ ☐
Have self-esteem and self-management . . . . . ☑ ☐
Be sociable . . . . ☑ ☐
Be fair, honest, and sincere . . . . ☑ ☐

Work Styles

Licensed practical nurses must work well with people. LPNs are part of health care teams. They work with doctors, registered nurses, and other professionals. LPNs must be able to follow orders. They must be able to work both with and without direct supervision.

LPNs must be able to handle stress. They may work closely with patients who are uncomfortable, in pain, or even near death. LPNs must be able to handle the emotional stress of working with these patients. Nurses must continue to work even when they feel sad, tired, or under pressure.

LPNs must accept some hazards. They may be exposed to chemicals or radiation. Radiation's powerful rays are used in the treatment of some diseases and to take X rays. An X ray is a photograph of the inside of a person's body. LPNs wear protective clothing to shield themselves against radiation. LPNs may be exposed to infectious diseases. These diseases can easily pass from one person to another. LPNs protect themselves by wearing masks that cover their mouths and noses. They also wear rubber gloves to protect their hands and skin.

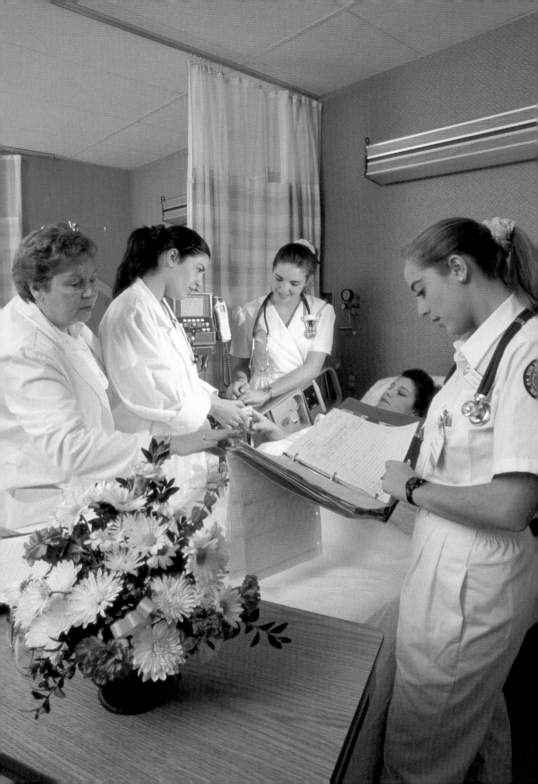

Chapter 4

Preparing for the Career

People who want to become licensed practical nurses must complete approved nursing programs. These programs take about one to two years to complete. Students also may be required to take an exam after they complete school.

High School Education

High school students who want to become licensed practical nurses should take a variety of classes. These should include a range of science and math courses. Students should take communication classes such as English and speech. They also should take computer classes.

Students may benefit from participation in school and community groups. These groups

People who want to become licensed practical nurses must complete nursing programs.

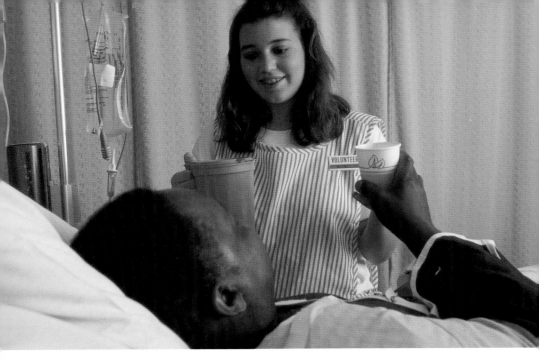

High school students can gain experience by volunteering at medical facilities.

include 4-H and scouting. Such groups help students learn how to work with others.

High school students can gain experience through volunteer work at medical facilities. Students can do work without pay at hospitals, long-term care facilities, and clinics. Student volunteers may assist LPNs. These volunteers sometimes are called candy stripers. Student volunteers may be able to observe jobs LPNs perform. This helps students learn if they want to become LPNs someday.

Post-Secondary Education

People must complete nursing programs to become licensed practical nurses. Many vocational, technical, and trade schools offer nursing programs. These programs also are offered at community colleges, hospitals, and health agencies. Most practical nursing programs take about a year to complete. But programs at community colleges may take about two years. In the United States, students receive associate's degrees after graduation.

In Canada, students must complete practical nursing programs at community colleges. Most programs take 12 to 14 months to complete. In Canada, students receive a diploma in practical nursing after graduation.

Practical nursing programs include both classroom study and clinical practice. Classroom study covers basic nursing concepts and subjects related to patient care. These subjects include anatomy, physiology, and pediatrics. Anatomy is the study of the parts that make up living things. Physiology is the study of how those parts work. Pediatrics is the medical care of children.

In clinical practice, students learn how to work with patients by studying patient care. Students first practice nursing procedures using

High
School
Diploma

Associate's
Degree

mannequins. Students practice giving shots to these human-like dolls. Students also practice taking other students' vital signs. After much practice, students visit real patients. Students perform clinical rotations. In clinical rotations, LPNs work on different floors or units of health care facilities.

Many practical nursing programs enable practical nursing graduates to continue their education. These nurses eventually can complete courses to become registered nurses.

Licensing/Registering

In the United States, students must pass a licensing exam after graduating from a nursing program. The written test is called the National Council Licensure Examination for Practical Nurses.

In the United States, all states require practical nurses to be licensed. LPNs must renew their license every two years.

In Canada, students must pass a registering exam after they graduate from a nursing program. The exam is a written test called the National Licensed Practical Nurses Exam. In Quebec, students do not take the national test. They take a provincial test offered by the Ordre des infirmières et infirmiers auxiliaires du Québec. This is the Quebec regulatory association for LPNs.

LPNs in Canada must annually register with the regulatory body in the province where they work. LPNs must pay an annual fee to the regulatory body. They also must indicate how much they have worked during a set period of time. But the rules are different in the provinces of British Columbia and Ontario. Here, LPNs do not indicate how much they have worked. Instead, they participate in an assessment program to ensure the quality of working LPNs. An assessment is the judgment of someone's skills.

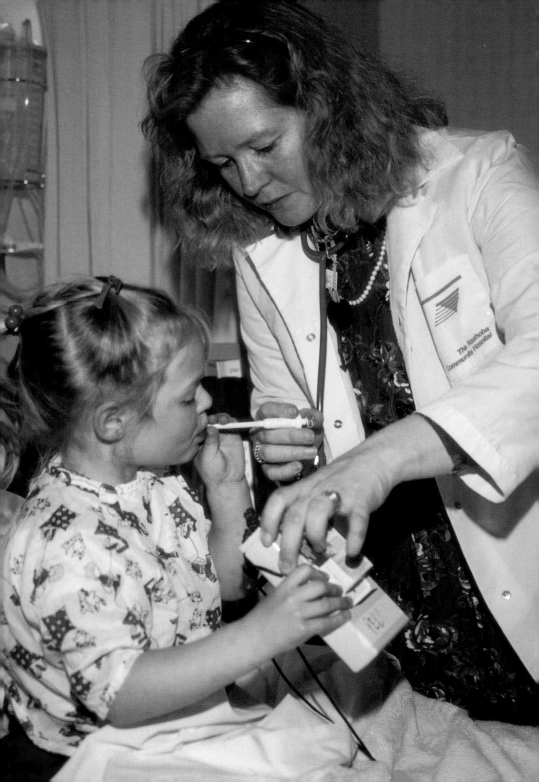

Chapter 5

The Market

Licensed practical nurses work in many different health care facilities. Most LPNs work in hospitals, clinics, and long-term care facilities. Some LPNs work in the hospital or clinic where they completed their training. Other LPNs work in private homes, government agencies, and schools.

Salary

Salaries of licensed practical nurses vary depending on where LPNs work. Salaries also vary with LPNs' experience.

In the United States, LPNs earn between $16,536 and $34,996 per year. The average yearly salary for full-time LPNs is about $20,000 to $29,000. LPNs in long-term care facilities earn about $22,000 to $28,000 per year.

LPNs work in many different health care facilities.

Private duty nurses treat patients at their homes.

In Canada, LPNs earn between $18,400 and about $36,400 per year. The average yearly salary for full-time LPNs in Canada is about $30,800.

Job Outlook
In the United States, licensed practical nurses will experience job growth. The number of jobs is expected to grow faster than average. Several factors will cause this growth. One factor is that the U.S. population is aging. As people age, they tend to have more health problems. LPNs will be needed to provide care for these people. The health

care industry also is growing. LPNs will be in demand as this industry grows.

In the future, LPNs who want jobs in hospitals may face competition. There are expected to be fewer hospital positions available than the number of new LPNs.

LPNs will have many job opportunities at long-term care facilities in the future. More LPNs will be needed as more patients stay at these facilities. More older or disabled people are being moved from hospitals to long-term care facilities. Hospital treatment is very expensive. Long-term care facilities can care for patients at lower costs.

The need for private duty nurses also is expected to grow. More elderly patients are choosing to live at home. These patients hire private duty nurses to live with them or assist them. Also, more patients are choosing to leave hospitals and recover in their homes.

Jobs for LPNs will likely increase in other areas as well. LPNs will find work at residential care facilities. These facilities also are known as group homes. Residential care facilities provide homes for people who are developmentally disabled. LPNs also will continue to find jobs in doctor's offices and clinics.

In Canada, the job outlook for LPNs is fair. In the future, hospitals will need workers with specialized skills. Registered nurses will be needed for these jobs. But overall, jobs will likely increase in the health and social services areas in Canada. Jobs also will likely increase in private health practices and medical laboratories.

Advancement Opportunities

Licensed practical nurses with experience can advance by becoming supervisors. LPNs usually need several years of experience to become supervisors. These supervisors oversee the work of nursing assistants and nurse's aides.

LPNs also can advance by getting more education and training. Some LPNs become registered nurses. LPNs must complete two additional years of training at a college or university to become an RN. People receive a bachelor's degree after completing a nursing program at a college or university. Other LPNs complete a shorter education program and specialize in a nursing field. These fields include areas such as surgery or therapy.

LPNs must keep their skills current. They must learn about new treatments and medicines. LPNs

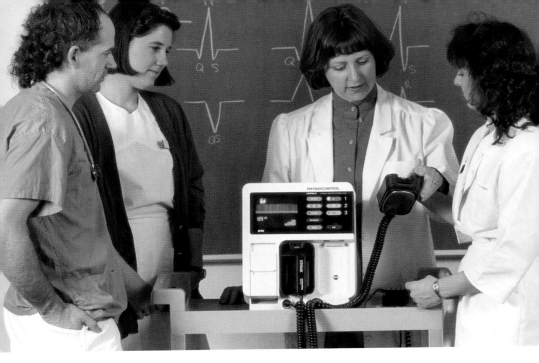

Some licensed practical nurses go back to school.

may learn new information through professional organizations or on-the-job training. Many LPNs attend conferences. Some LPNs read professional publications. These magazines and journals contain the latest news about the nursing profession.

There will continue to be a need for LPNs. These nurses will be needed at hospitals, clinics, long-term care facilities, and private homes. People will always have health care needs. LPNs will continue to help care for those people.

Words to Know

artery (AR-tuh-ree)—a tube that carries blood from the heart to other parts of the body

blood pressure (BLUHD PRESH-ur)—the force of blood pulsing against the walls of the arteries when the heart is pumping and when it is at rest

charge nurse (CHARJ NURSS)—the nurse in charge of a particular floor or unit of a hospital, long-term care facility, or other health care setting

hygiene (HYE-jeen)—actions people do to stay clean and healthy

long-term care facility (LAWNG-TURM KAIR fuh-SIL-uh-tee)—a place where patients go for weeks, months, or years to receive medical treatment or live; a nursing home is a long-term care facility.

resident (REZ-uh-duhnt)—someone staying in a long-term care facility

respiration (ress-puh-RAY-shuhn)—the process of taking in oxygen and sending out carbon dioxide

rounds (ROUNDS)—a regular route or course of action of a doctor in a hospital or long-term care facility

syringe (suh-RINJ)—a tube with a plunger and a hollow needle; licensed practical nurses use syringes to inject medicine into patients.

vital signs (VYE-tuhl SINES)—signs of life; pulse rate, temperature, breathing, and blood pressure are vital signs.

X ray (EKS-ray)—a photograph of the inside of a person's body

To Learn More

Frederickson, Keville. *Opportunities in Nursing Careers.* VGM Opportunities Series. Lincolnwood, Ill.: VGM Career Horizons, 1996.

James, Robert. *Nurses: People Who Care for Our Health.* Vero Beach, Fla.: Rourke, 1995.

Lindberg, Janice B., Mary Love Hunter, and Ann Z. Kruszewski. *Introduction to Nursing: Concepts, Issues, and Opportunities.* Philadelphia: Lippincott, 1998.

Sacks, Terence J. *Careers in Nursing.* VGM Professional Careers Series. Lincolnwood, Ill.: VGM Career Horizons, 1998.

Vallano, Annette. *Careers in Nursing: Managing Your Future in the Changing World of Healthcare.* New York: Simon & Schuster, 1999.

Useful Addresses

Canadian Nurses Association
50 Driveway
Ottawa, ON K2P 1E2
Canada

National Association for Practical Nurse Education and Service, Inc.
1400 Spring Street
Suite 330
Silver Spring, MD 20910

National Federation of Licensed Practical Nurses, Inc.
893 U.S. Highway 70 West
Suite 202
Garner, NC 27529

National League for Nursing
61 Broadway
New York, NY 10006

Internet Sites

American Nurses Association
http://www.nursingworld.org

Canadian Nurses Association
http://www.cna-nurses.ca

KidsHealth
http://www.kidshealth.org

National League for Nursing
http://www.nln.org

Occupational Outlook Handbook—Licensed Practical Nurses
http://www.bls.gov/oco/ocos102.htm

Your Gross and Cool Body
http://www.yucky.com/body

Index

DATE DUE

AUG 2 9 2000			
MAY 2 3 2001			
JE 14 '04			